DK READERS is a compelling program for beginning readers, designed in conjunction with leading literacy experts, including Dr. Linda Gambrell, Distinguished Professor of Education at Clemson University. Dr. Gambrell has served as President of the National Reading Conference, the College Reading Association, and the International Reading Association.

Beautiful illustrations and superb full-color photographs combine with engaging, easy-to-read stories to offer a fresh approach to each subject in the series. Each DK READER is guaranteed to capture a child's interest while developing his or her reading skills, general knowledge, and love of reading.

The five levels of DK READERS are aimed at different reading abilities, enabling you to choose the books that are exactly right for your child:

Pre-level 1: Learning to read
Level 1: Beginning to read
Level 2: Beginning to read alone
Level 3: Reading alone
Level 4: Proficient readers

The "normal" age at which a child begins to read can be anywhere from three to eight years old. Adult participation through the lower levels is very helpful for providing encouragement, discussing storylines, and sounding out unfamiliar words.

No matter which level you select, you can be sure that you are helping your child learn to read, then read to learn!

W9-DGU-518

LONDON, NEW YORK, MUNICH,
MELBOURNE, and DELHI

For DK/BradyGames

Title Manager Tim Fitzpatrick
Cover Designer Tim Amrhein
Production Designer Wil Cruz
Vice President & Publisher Mike Degler
Editor-In-Chief H. Leigh Davis
Licensing Manager Christian Sumner
Marketing Manager Katie Hemlock
Digital Publishing Manager Tim Cox
Operations Manager Stacey Beheler

Reading Consultant Linda B. Gambrell, Ph.D.

For WWE

Global Publishing Manager Steve Pantaleo
Photo Department Frank Vitucci,
Josh Tottenham, Jamie Nelson, Mike Moran,
JD Sestito, Melissa Halladay, Lea Girard
Legal Lauren Dienes-Middlen

DK/BradyGAMES
800 East 96th St., 3rd floor
Indianapolis, IN 46240

14 15 16 10 9 8 7 6 5 4 3 2 1

ISBN: 978-1-4654-2295-8 (Paperback)
ISBN: 978-1-4654-2296-5 (Hardback)

Printed and bound by Lake Book

The publisher would like to thank the following for their kind
permission to reproduce their photographs:
All photos courtesy WWE Entertainment, Inc.

All other images © Dorling Kindersley
For further information see: www.dkimages.com

Discover more at
www.dk.com

DK READERS

BEGINNING TO READ ALONE 2

The Rock

Written by Steve Pantaleo

The Rock is the most electrifying man in all of entertainment. He is also the most charismatic Superstar in WWE history. Born Dwayne Johnson, The Rock is an eight-time WWE Champion and a Hollywood sensation. Descending from the legendary Anoa'i family, The Rock seemed destined for greatness.

Both his father and grandfather were Superstars before him, making him WWE's first third-generation Superstar. However, The Rock needed unlimited grit and willpower to achieve his amazing success.

The Rock Stats
Height: 6' 5"
Weight: 260 lbs.
Hometown: Miami, FL
Signature Moves: Rock Bottom, People's Elbow

Long before becoming a WWE Superstar, Dwayne Johnson was a standout football player. In college, he played for the Miami Hurricanes and was part of the 1991 National Championship team. He excelled in football, but his heart was set on another goal, one that was in his blood: WWE.

Dwayne Johnson's father, Rocky Johnson, trained him rigorously.

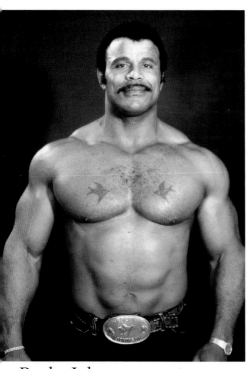

Rocky Johnson

He wanted his son to know exactly how tough life in the ring could be. Choosing to honor his father and grandfather, the budding star debuted in WWE as Rocky Maivia. This combined his father's name with that of his grandfather, High Chief Peter Maivia.

Rocky Maivia debuted in the world famous Madison Square Garden. His performance was impressive, sparking his *Survivor Series* team to victory. Soon after, he enjoyed a brief reign as the Intercontinental Champion. Despite this strong start to his career, fans quickly soured on the clean cut Maivia, showering him with scornful jeers.

The Rock's Electrifying MSG Moments

Survivor Series 1996: Rocky Maivia dominates in his debut match.

Royal Rumble 2000: The Rock wins the 30-man *Royal Rumble* Match.

WrestleMania XX, 2004: The Rock n' Sock Connection reunites.

Survivor Series 2011: Fans chant, "You still got it!" in his return match, recognizing that The Rock had not lost a step.

Maivia did not let the hostile crowds discourage him. Instead, he joined the villainous Nation of Domination and quickly unseated Faarooq as the group's leader. This bold new attitude propelled him to a long-lasting reign as the Intercontinental Champion.

Now known as The Rock, he ed The Nation against rivals D-Generation X and Stone Cold Steve Austin.

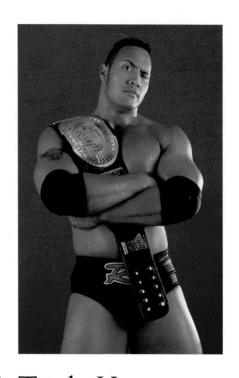

DX's Triple H beat him for the Intercontinental Title at *SummerSlam* 1998, but The Rock's momentum was still building.

The WWE brass knew The Rock had the spirit of a champion. Little did the WWE Universe know, The People's Champion was already aligned with WWE boss Mr. McMahon. This secret was revealed when he won his first WWE Championship in a 14-man tournament at *Survivor Series* 1998.

As The Corporate Champion, The Rock had some of the most intense battles in history with rival Mankind. He also headlined *WrestleMania* for the first time, colliding with Stone Cold Steve Austin.

"Rock Bottom"

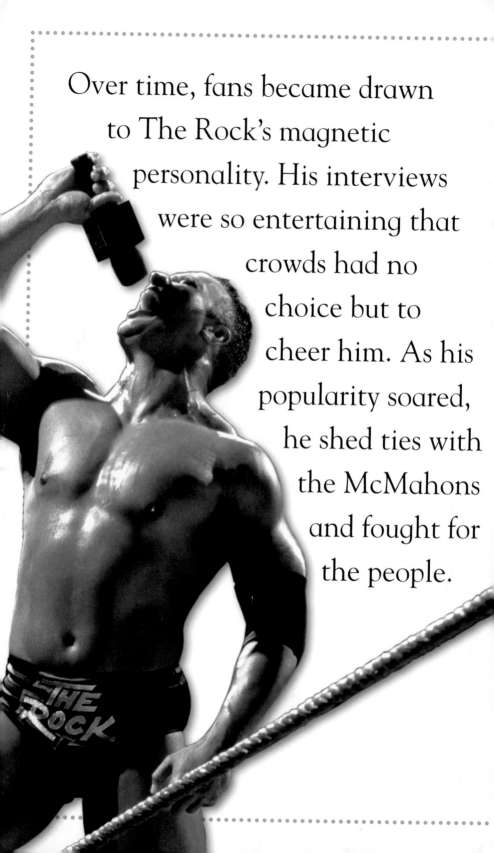

Over time, fans became drawn to The Rock's magnetic personality. His interviews were so entertaining that crowds had no choice but to cheer him. As his popularity soared, he shed ties with the McMahons and fought for the people.

He even embraced Mankind, forming the Rock n' Sock Connection. Known for their memorable comedic timing, the unlikely duo also clicked in the ring.  They won three World Tag Team Championships before The Rock went solo. Soon after, The Brahma Bull won the 2000 *Royal Rumble* and eventually defeated Triple H for the WWE Championship. The Rock's career skyrocketed.

The Rock Says...

"Know your role and shut your mouth!"

"If you smell what The Rock is cookin'!"

"It doesn't matter what your name is!"

"I will layeth the smacketh down!"

"Finally... The Rock has come back!"

"You will go one-on-one with the Great One!"

"Just bring it!"

"The millions (AND MILLIONS!)
of The Rock's fans..."

During this dramatic rise, The Rock pinned Kurt Angle for his sixth WWE Championship, punching his ticket to *WrestleMania X-7*. On WWE's grandest stage, he suffered his most crushing loss when Stone Cold defeated him with assistance from Mr. McMahon.

However, The Great One would not be down for long. He helped save WWE from a hostile takeover in 2001 by winning the WCW Championship from Booker T. Later, he led Team WWE to victory against the WCW/ECW Alliance, crushing the invasion.

In February 2002, The Rock challenged the immortal Hulk Hogan to go one-on-one at *WrestleMania X8*. The match would feature the most legendary Superstars from two different eras competing against each other. Only in WWE can two generations collide in one epic encounter.

When the two icons stared each other down, the crowd went wild,  alternating chants for both The Rock and The Hulkster.

No one was sitting. Feeding off
his Hulkamaniacs, Hogan
punished The Rock with a Big
Boot and patented Leg Drop.
However, The Rock recovered to
hit a Rock Bottom and win the
historic match.

The two competitors showed proper respect by shaking hands after the match. The win boosted Rock toward another title opportunity at *Vengeance* 2002. There, he beat both Kurt Angle and Undertaker for his record-setting seventh WWE Championship.

The Rock had nearly accomplished everything he could in the ring. So, he broadened his horizons, starring in movies. He also showcased his musical talent, performing humorous "Rock concerts" for WWE crowds. Still, one goal had eluded him: defeating Stone Cold Steve Austin at *WrestleMania.*

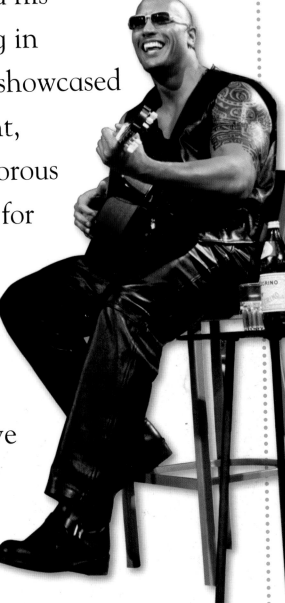

In two previous attempts, he failed to defeat his most bitter rival on the grandest stage. *WrestleMania XIX* would be his last chance. He needed this win to cement his legacy, but Austin was tough as nails. The encounter was fierce. Both Superstars used several finishing moves hoping to end the match, but neither would give up. It took an astounding three Rock Bottoms to keep Stone Cold down for the three-count, but The Rock had done it. He notched a win, ending one of the greatest rivalries of all time.

After defeating Austin, The Rock focused on electrifying the silver screen. He backed up his previous Hollywood success with lead performances in *Walking Tall* and *Be Cool*. Over seven years, Dwayne "The Rock" Johnson evolved into a mainstream celebrity.

He only made brief appearances in WWE, and the millions (and millions) of WWE fans missed seeing him compete.

However, the same charisma that made him the People's Champ shined through in more than a dozen films.

The Rock in Movies

2014
Hercules

2013
Fast & Furious 6
Pain & Gain
Empire State
G.I. Joe: Retaliation
Snitch

2012
Journey 2:
  The Mysterious Island

2011
Fast Five

2010
Faster
The Other Guys
Tooth Fairy

2009
Race to
  Witch Mountain

2008
Get Smart

2007
The Game Plan

2006
Gridiron Gang
Southland Tales

2005
Doom
Be Cool

2004
Walking Tall

2003
The Rundown

2002
The Scorpion King

2001
Longshot
The Mummy Returns

In February 2011, WWE made a blockbuster announcement. Finally, The Rock was back in WWE! Promising to once again "bring it," he traded insults with WWE's biggest current star, John Cena. At *WrestleMania XXVII*, he dropped the Cenation leader with a Rock Bottom, costing Cena his match.

For over a year, their rivalry became increasingly hostile. At *WrestleMania XXVIII*, in The Rock's hometown of Miami, the stage was finally set for a once in a lifetime clash.

Cena gave The Great One all he could handle. The combatants were equal in strength, skill, and desire. Cena tried to finish The Rock with his own People's Elbow, but The Rock sprang to his feet just in time. He delivered a thunderous Rock Bottom and pinned Cena to win another classic battle of generations.

The Rock vowed to once again become WWE Champion. It had been ten years since he last held the celebrated prize, which was currently around the waist of CM Punk. Known as the "Best in the World," Punk was as dominant as he was brash. For 434 days, no one could beat him for the title.

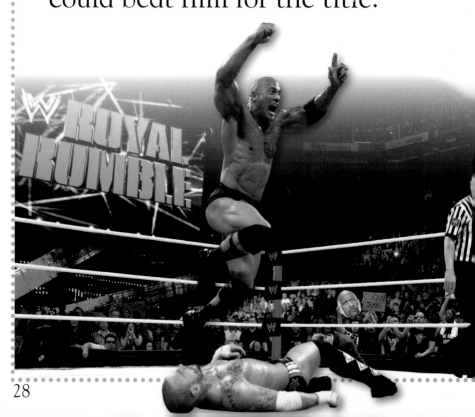

With his mother in attendance, The Rock faced Punk at *Royal Rumble* 2013. The competitors fought fearlessly. After an ambush

by The Shield nearly derailed the contest, The Rock dug down. He countered Punk move for move, then connected with a People's Elbow for the win. His eighth WWE Championship was the perfect capstone to a miraculous career.

There is no telling what The Rock will do next. He still trains extremely hard, just like his father taught him decades ago. His regimen includes intense weight training and cardio to build strength and stamina. He also follows a strict diet, eating lots of protein and avoiding too many sweets.

The Rock Facts

- The term "SmackDown" was first used by The Rock before it became the title of one of WWE's weekly shows in 1999.

- In college, The Rock shared defensive line duties with NFL legend Warren Sapp.

- The Rock has appeared on several TV shows, including *Saturday Night Live*. He also portrayed his own father in an episode of *That '70s Show*.

- The Rock was Forbes top grossing actor in 2013. That means people spent more money to see his movies ($1.3 billion dollars!) than any other actor.

With this strong work ethic, The Rock will be ready for whatever challenge lies ahead. You can guarantee that no one—and The Rock means *no one*—will ever

lay the smackdown in sports and entertainment quite like Dwayne "The Rock" Johnson.

STAY FIT, EAT HEALTHY & CHALLENGE YOUR BRAIN
WITH WWE KIDS MAGAZINE

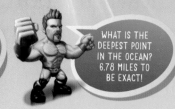

DRINK LOTS OF WATER. STAYING HYDRATED IS THE KEY TO STAYING HEALTHY!

WHAT IS THE DEEPEST POINT IN THE OCEAN? 6.78 MILES TO BE EXACT!

USE YOUR PALM TO MEASURE HOW MUCH LEAN MEAT YOU SHOULD EAT DAILY!

TO SUBSCRIBE GO TO: **MAG.WWEKIDS.CO**

5